CREEP, LEAP, CRUNCH!

A Food Chain Story

For Dad, for teaching me wonder and Latin roots
—J.J.S.

For Jasper and River
—C.S.N.

CREEP, LEAP, CRUNCH!

A Food Chain Story

words by
Jody Jensen Shaffer

art by
Christopher Silas Neal

Alfred A. Knopf
New York

There was a blue sky with a bright shining sun,

a glorious, life-giving, fiery sun.

The day had begun.

There was a huge forest
of grasses and trees
that blew in the cool
of a blustery breeze.

The plants made their food
with the help of the sun,
the glorious, life-giving, fiery sun.
The day had begun.

There was a quick cricket

awake in the grass.

That cricket was fast!

He nibbled sweet grass.

The cricket munched grass

far beneath the tall trees

that blew in the cool

of a blustery breeze.

The plants made their food

with the help of the sun,

the glorious, life-giving, fiery sun.

The day had begun.

There was a brown deer mouse
that spied the quick cricket.
From out of his thicket,
he pounced on that cricket.

The mouse from the thicket
gobbled the cricket.
The cricket munched grass
far beneath the tall trees
that blew in the cool
of a blustery breeze.
The plants made their food
with the help of the sun,
the glorious, life-giving, fiery sun.
The day had begun.

There was a red milk snake
that spotted the mouse.
He slid from his house,
and he sprang at that mouse.

The snake slid and slithered
and swallowed the mouse.
The mouse from the thicket
gobbled the cricket.
The cricket munched grass
far beneath the tall trees
that blew in the cool
of a blustery breeze.
The plants made their food
with the help of the sun,
the glorious, life-giving, fiery sun.
The day was half done.

There was a red hawk

peering down at the snake.

Make no mistake,

he scooped up that snake!

The fast-diving hawk

swooped down on the snake.

The snake slid and slithered

and swallowed the mouse.

The mouse from the thicket

gobbled the cricket.

The cricket munched grass

far beneath the tall trees

that blew in the cool

of a blustery breeze.

The plants made their food

with the help of the sun,

the glorious, life-giving, fiery sun.

The day was half done.

There was a red fox

that trapped the red hawk.

He crept off a rock,

and he cornered that hawk.

The creeping red fox

sneaked up on the hawk.

Make no mistake,

the hawk caught the snake.

The snake slid and slithered

and swallowed the mouse.

The mouse from the thicket

gobbled the cricket.

The cricket munched grass

far beneath the tall trees

that blew in the cool

of a blustery breeze.

The plants made their food

with the help of the sun,

the glorious, life-giving, fiery sun.

The day was half done.

There was a black bear

that tracked down the fox.

Sleepy but hungry,

she found that red fox.

The bear sniffed the air,

and she followed the fox.

The creeping red fox

sneaked up on the hawk.

Make no mistake,

the hawk caught the snake.

The snake slid and slithered

and swallowed the mouse.

The mouse from the thicket

gobbled the cricket.

The cricket munched grass

far beneath the tall trees

that blew in the cool

of a blustery breeze.

The plants made their food

with the help of the sun,

the glorious, life-giving, slow-sinking sun.

This day was now done.

But some days . . .

the cricket that's fast

hops away from the mouse,

the pouncing brown mouse

scrambles past the red snake,

the slithery snake

slides beneath the swift hawk,

the swooping red hawk

zooms above the red fox,

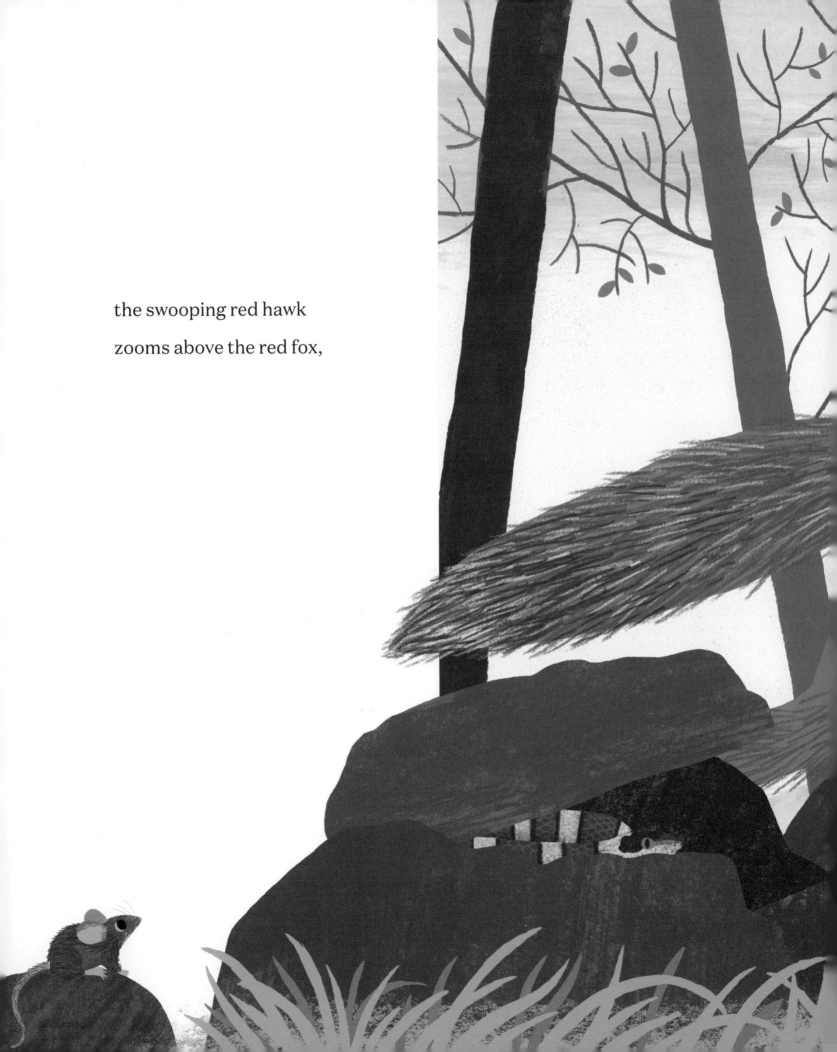

the bushy-tailed fox

sneaks around the black bear,

and the hungry black bear

munches flowers and seeds . . .

. . . all that she needs.

Glossary

food chain: A food chain is a sequence of organisms in an ecosystem where the smallest species is fed upon by a larger species until the chain ends at the largest consumer. In this book, the food chain begins with the sun. Through a process called **photosynthesis**, the energy in the sun— together with water, carbon dioxide, and nutrients from the soil—helps plants make their own food. Plants are **producers**. A cricket eats grass to gain energy. A mouse eats the cricket for the same reason, and so on. The animals in this food chain are **consumers**.

temperate deciduous forest: This food chain occurs in a temperate deciduous forest. These forests contain many trees that lose their leaves in the winter. Elm, oak, and maple trees are deciduous.

black bear: Black bears are large mammals at the top of their food chain. During the fall, as they prepare for a long winter of sleep (they don't truly hibernate), black bears can double their weight. Black bears eat plants, berries, nuts, and other animals. When spring comes, they are hungry! Black bears may be black, gray, cinnamon, or white.

cricket: Crickets are jumping insects. Males rub their forewings together to make loud chirping noises. This is called **stridulation**. Crickets live under logs and in grassy areas and trees. They are omnivores and eat both plants and animals.

deer mouse: The deer mouse is a small brown mouse with large ears, a white tummy, and a long, smooth tail. It lives in hedgerows, thickets, and fields. It eats seeds, fruits, and invertebrates. Its predators include owls, foxes, and snakes. A deer mouse is different from a mouse you might find in your house. A house mouse is brown or gray all over and has an almost hairless tail.

red fox: The red fox has a rusty red coat with white under its chin and on its belly. The tip of its bushy tail is also white. Foxes stalk their prey by creeping as close to it as possible and then chasing it down.

red milk snake: This snake is white or light tan with orange or red markings bordered by black. Its belly is white and black. It lives under rocks on hillsides and in glades. It can grow up to two feet long. It kills its prey by squeezing it.

red-tailed hawk: The red-tailed hawk is a raptor (bird of prey) that can grow up to twenty-two inches long, with a wingspan of four feet. These stocky, powerful birds have excellent eyesight and can spot mice from one hundred feet away.

THIS IS A BORZOI BOOK PUBLISHED BY ALFRED A. KNOPF

Text copyright © 2023 by Jody Jensen Shaffer
Jacket art and interior illustrations copyright © 2023 by Christopher Silas Neal

All rights reserved. Published in the United States by Alfred A. Knopf, an imprint of
Random House Children's Books, a division of Penguin Random House LLC, New York.

Knopf, Borzoi Books, and the colophon are registered trademarks of Penguin Random House LLC.

Visit us on the Web! rhcbooks.com

Educators and librarians, for a variety of teaching tools, visit us at RHTeachersLibrarians.com

Library of Congress Cataloging-in-Publication Data is available upon request.
ISBN 978-0-593-56552-0 (trade) — ISBN 978-0-593-56553-7 (lib. bdg.) — ISBN 978-0-593-56554-4 (ebook)

The text of this book is set in Domaine.
The illustrations were created in mixed media and finished digitally.
Book design by Taline Boghosian

MANUFACTURED IN CHINA   10 9 8 7 6 5 4 3 2 1   First Edition